WACKY COMPARISONS
HOW LONG?
WACKY WAYS TO COMPARE LENGTH

by Jessica Gunderson

illustrated by Igor Sinkovec

How long is a **SHIP**? Or a **SNAKE** that slithers?

Is either as long as the **MISSISSIPPI RIVER**?

A **SHARK'S TOOTH**, a **DINO** long gone—
look inside to see **HOW LONG**!

PICTURE WINDOW BOOKS
a capstone imprint

Listen up, elephant,
no ifs, ands, or buts,

your **TRUNK** is as long as
42 PEANUTS.

1 trunk = 7 feet (2.1 meters); 1 peanut = 2 inches (5 centimeters)

1 FOOTBALL FIELD is just as long

as **960** SANDWICHES joined in song.

1 field = 360 ft. (110 m); 1 sandwich = 4½ in. (11 cm)

3 POINTY HUMAN TEETH, it's the truth,

are nearly the length of

1 GREAT WHITE SHARK TOOTH.

1 shark tooth = 2½ in. (6 cm); 1 human tooth = 7/8 in. (22 millimeters)

7

How long was **APATOSAURUS**, head to tail?

Along its back **30** SKATEBOARDERS sail.

1 apatosaurus = 74 ft. (23 m); 1 skateboard = 2½ ft. (76 cm)

7 STICKS OF LICORICE stuck together

equal the length of

1 PEACOCK FEATHER.

1 feather = 5 ft. (1.5 m); 1 licorice stick = 8 in. (20 cm)

A ROCKET TO THE MOON is a **3**-DAY RIDE.

How long for a

CAR DRIVING 65?

153 DAYS

(at 65 miles [105 kilometers] per hour)

distance to the moon = 238,855 miles (384,400 km)
rocket speed = 6,635 miles (10,678 km) per hour

How many **RATS** does it take to make

1 snake = 20 ft. (6.1 m); 1 rat = 1½ ft. (46 cm)

1 ROYAL CRUISE SHIP stretches out to sea.

It's the length of

170 MATTRESSES

fit for a queen.

10,961 CRUISE SHIPS,

you can see,

are just as long as

1 MISSISSIPPI.

An EAGLE spreads its wings so wide—

the length of **13 DOLLAR BILLS** side by side.

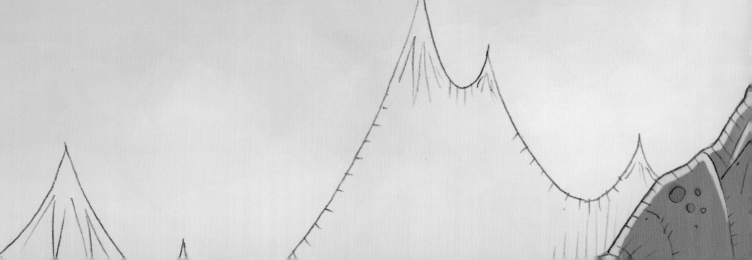

1 eagle = 6 ft., 10 in. (2.1 m); 1 bill = 6 1/8 in. (16 cm)

The **GOLDEN GATE BRIDGE**
from shore to shore

equals the length of
180 LADDER TRUCKS, and no more.

HOW LONG, you wonder,
till we reach the end?
IT'S HERE! This book is done, my friend.

1 bridge = 1.7 miles (2.7 km); 1 truck = 50 ft. (15 m)

READ MORE

Adamson, Thomas K., and Heather Adamson.
How Do You Measure Length and Distance?
Measure It! Mankato, Minn.: Capstone Press, 2011.

Karapetkova, Holly. *Pounds, Feet, and Inches.*
Concepts. Vero Beach, Fla.: Rourke Pub., 2010.

Vogel, Julia. *Measuring Length.* Mankato, Minn.:
The Child's World, 2013.

INTERNET SITES

FactHound offers a safe, fun way to find Internet sites related to this book. All of the sites on FactHound have been researched by our staff.

Here's all you do:

Visit *www.facthound.com*

Type in this code: 9781404883246

Super-cool stuff! Check out projects, games and lots more at
www.capstonekids.com

Special thanks to our adviser, Terry Flaherty, PhD, Professor of English, Minnesota State University, Mankato, for his expertise.

Editor: Jill Kalz
Designer: Ashlee Suker
Art Director: Nathan Gassman
Production Specialist: Eric Manske
The illustrations in this book were created digitally.

Picture Window Books are published by Capstone,
1710 Roe Crest Drive, North Mankato, Minnesota 56003
www.capstonepub.com

Library of Congress Cataloging-in-Publication Data
Gunderson, Jessica.
  How long? : wacky ways to compare length / by Jessica Gunderson; illustrated by Igor Sinkovec.
     pages cm. — (Wacky comparisons)
  Summary: "Compares various long objects to shorter objects in unique, illustrated ways"—Provided by publisher.
  Audience: K to grade 3.
  Includes bibliographical references.
  ISBN 978-1-4048-8324-6 (library binding)
  ISBN 978-1-4795-1914-9 (paperback)
  ISBN 978-1-4795-1910-1 (eBook PDF)
1. Length measurement—Juvenile literature. 2. Comparison (Philosophy)—Juvenile literature. I. Sinkovec, Igor, illustrator. II. Title.

QC102.G86 2014
530.8—dc23   2013012151

Printed in the United States of America in North Mankato, Minnesota.
022014   008009R

LOOK FOR ALL THE BOOKS IN THE SERIES:

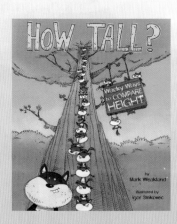